Pennies on my Eyes

Dr Jane Potter is Reader in Arts at the Oxford International Centre for Publishing at Oxford Brookes University. Her publications include *Boys in Khaki, Girls in Print: Women's Literary Responses to the Great War, 1914–1918* (Oxford University Press, 2005), *Wilfred Owen: An Illustrated Life* (Bodleian Library Publishing, 2014), and, with Carol Acton, *Working in a World of Hurt: Trauma and Resilience in the Narratives of Medical Personnel in War Zones* (Manchester University Press, 2015). With Jon Stallworthy, she edited *Three Poets of the First World War: Ivor Gurney, Isaac Rosenberg and Wilfred Owen* (Penguin, 2011), and is currently editing a new edition of Wilfred Owen's selected letters for Oxford University Press.

Two Rivers Classic Poems

Pennies on my Eyes

Poems by Wilfred Owen
With an Afterword by Jane Potter

TWO
RIVERS
PRESS

First published in the UK in 2018 by Two Rivers Press
7 Denmark Road, Reading RG1 5PA
www.tworiverspress.com

ISBN 978-1-909747-44-9

1 2 3 4 5 6 7 8 9

Two Rivers Press is represented in the UK by Inpress Ltd
and distributed by NBNi.

Cover design and illustration by Sally Castle
Text design by Nadja Guggi and typeset in Janson and Parisine

Printed and bound in Great Britain by Gomer Press, Ceredigion

Publisher's Acknowledgements

Two Rivers Press is grateful to the Dunsden Owen Association for supporting
this project, particularly with respect to publicity and the book launch.

The Dunsden Owen Association (www.owenindunsden.org) was set up in
2013 by a diverse group of locals, in recognition of the seminal years the radical
war poet spent in the small village of Dunsden as lay assistant to the local vicar.
Using Owen's own letters written at this time, the DOA has created a self-guided
walking trail (with an accompanying smartphone app and printed leaflet) that
charts the poet's Dunsden years, taking in the major landmarks of his time spent
here. The DOA also organises thought-provoking community events that promote
Owen's poetry, and which remain true to the spirit of his work.

The inscription reproduced on the inside covers is from a prayer book given
to Wilfred Owen by Canon WHF Robson – famous in the region as a superb
speaker with a saintly, magnetic personality. The book is now in the possession
of the DOA.

Contents

Dulce et Decorum Est

Bent double, like old beggars under sacks,
Knock-kneed, coughing like hags, we cursed through sludge,
Till on the haunting flares we turned our backs,
And towards our distant rest began to trudge.
Men marched asleep. Many had lost their boots,
But limped on, blood-shod. All went lame; all blind;
Drunk with fatigue; deaf even to the hoots
Of gas-shells dropping softly behind.

Gas! GAS! Quick, boys!—An ecstasy of fumbling
Fitting the clumsy helmets just in time,
But someone still was yelling out and stumbling
And flound'ring like a man in fire or lime.—
Dim through the misty panes and thick green light,
As under a green sea, I saw him drowning.

In all my dreams before my helpless sight,
He plunges at me, guttering, choking, drowning.

If in some smothering dreams, you too could pace
Behind the wagon that we flung him in,
And watch the white eyes writhing in his face,
His hanging face, like a devil's sick of sin;
If you could hear, at every jolt, the blood
Come gargling from the froth-corrupted lungs,
Obscene as cancer, bitter as the cud
Of vile, incurable sores on innocent tongues,—
My friend, you would not tell with such high zest
To children ardent for some desperate glory,
The old Lie: *Dulce et decorum est
Pro patria mori.*

The Send-Off

Down the close, darkening lanes they sang their way
To the siding-shed,
And lined the train with faces grimly gay.

Their breasts were stuck all white with wreath and spray
As men's are, dead.

Dull porters watched them, and a casual tramp
Stood staring hard,
Sorry to miss them from the upland camp.
Then, unmoved, signals nodded, and a lamp
Winked to the guard.

So secretly, like wrongs hushed-up, they went.
They were not ours:
We never heard to which front these were sent.

Nor there if they yet mock what women meant
Who gave them flowers.

Shall they return to beatings of great bells
In wild trainloads?
A few, a few, too few for drums and yells,
May creep back, silent, to still village wells
Up half-known roads.

Illustration: Ahmad Alazami

Conscious

His fingers wake, and flutter up the bed.
His eyes come open with a pull of will,
Helped by the yellow may-flowers by his head.
A blind-cord drawls across the window-sill ...
How smooth the floor of the ward is! what a rug!
And who's that talking, somewhere out of sight?
Why are they laughing? What's inside that jug?
"Nurse! Doctor!" "Yes; all right, all right."
But sudden dusk bewilders all the air —
There seems no time to want a drink of water.
Nurse looks so far away. And everywhere
Music and roses burnt through crimson slaughter.
Cold; cold; he's cold; and yet so hot:
And there's no light to see the voices by —
No time to dream, and ask — he knows not what.

Illustration: Nadja Guggi

Anthem for Doomed Youth

What passing-bells for these who die as cattle?
    — Only the monstrous anger of the guns.
    Only the stuttering rifles' rapid rattle
Can patter out their hasty orisons.
No mockeries now for them; no prayers nor bells;
    Nor any voice of mourning save the choirs,—
The shrill, demented choirs of wailing shells;
    And bugles calling for them from sad shires.

What candles may be held to speed them all?
    Not in the hands of boys, but in their eyes
Shall shine the holy glimmers of goodbyes.
    The pallor of girls' brows shall be their pall;
Their flowers the tenderness of patient minds,
And each slow dusk a drawing-down of blinds.

Illustration: Martin Andrews

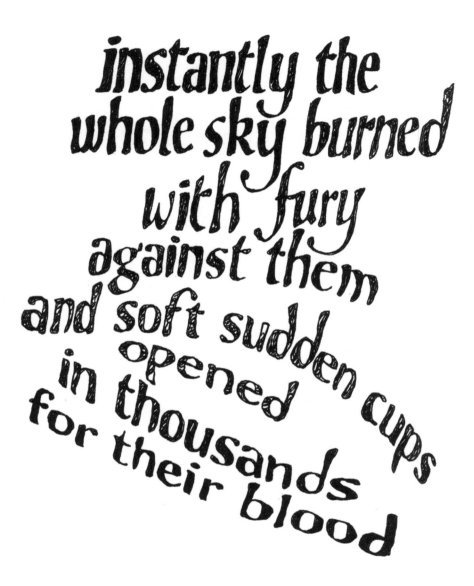

instantly the
whole sky burned
with fury
against them
and soft sudden cups
opened
in thousands
for their blood

Illustration: Geoff Sawers

Spring Offensive

Halted against the shade of a last hill,
They fed, and, lying easy, were at ease
And, finding comfortable chests and knees
Carelessly slept.
                But many there stood still
To face the stark, blank sky beyond the ridge,
Knowing their feet had come to the end of the world.
Marvelling they stood, and watched the long grass swirled
By the May breeze, murmurous with wasp and midge,
For though the summer oozed into their veins
Like the injected drug for their bones' pains,
Sharp on their souls hung the imminent line of grass,
Fearfully flashed the sky's mysterious glass.

Hour after hour they ponder the warm field—
And the far valley behind, where the buttercups
Had blessed with gold their slow boots coming up,
Where even the little brambles would not yield,
But clutched and clung to them like sorrowing hands;
They breathe like trees unstirred.
Till like a cold gust thrilled the little word
At which each body and its soul begird
And tighten them for battle. No alarms
Of bugles, no high flags, no clamorous haste—
Only a lift and flare of eyes that faced
The sun, like a friend with whom their love is done.
O larger shone that smile against the sun,—
Mightier than his whose bounty these have spurned.

So, soon they topped the hill, and raced together
Over an open stretch of herb and heather
Exposed. And instantly the whole sky burned
With fury against them; and soft sudden cups
Opened in thousands for their blood; and the green slopes
Chasmed and steepened sheer to infinite space.

Of them who running on that last high place
Leapt to swift unseen bullets, or went up
On the hot blast and fury of hell's upsurge,
Or plunged and fell away past this world's verge,
Some say God caught them even before they fell.
But what say such as from existence' brink
Ventured but drave too swift to sink.
The few who rushed in the body to enter hell,
And there out-fiending all its fiends and flames
With superhuman inhumanities,
Long-famous glories, immemorial shames—
And crawling slowly back, have by degrees
Regained cool peaceful air in wonder—
Why speak they not of comrades that went under?

Futility

Move him into the sun—
Gently its touch awoke him once,
At home, whispering of fields half-sown.
Always it woke him, even in France,
Until this morning and this snow.
If anything might rouse him now
The kind old sun will know.

Think how it wakes the seeds—
Woke once the clays of a cold star.
Are limbs, so dear-achieved, are sides
Full-nerved, still warm, too hard to stir?
Was it for this the clay grew tall?
—O what made fatuous sunbeams toil
To break earth's sleep at all?

Illustration: Nadja Guggi

11

Strange Meeting

It seemed that out of battle I escaped
Down some profound dull tunnel, long since scooped
Through granites which titanic wars had groined.

Yet also there encumbered sleepers groaned,
Too fast in thought or death to be bestirred.
Then, as I probed them, one sprang up, and stared
With piteous recognition in fixed eyes,
Lifting distressful hands, as if to bless.
And by his smile, I knew that sullen hall,—
By his dead smile I knew we stood in Hell.

With a thousand fears that vision's face was grained;
Yet no blood reached there from the upper ground,
And no guns thumped, or down the flues made moan.
"Strange friend," I said, "here is no cause to mourn."
"None," said that other, "save the undone years,
The hopelessness. Whatever hope is yours,
Was my life also; I went hunting wild
After the wildest beauty in the world,
Which lies not calm in eyes, or braided hair,
But mocks the steady running of the hour,
And if it grieves, grieves richlier than here.
For by my glee might many men have laughed,
And of my weeping something had been left,
Which must die now. I mean the truth untold,
The pity of war, the pity war distilled.
Now men will go content with what we spoiled.
Or, discontent, boil bloody, and be spilled.
They will be swift with swiftness of the tigress.
None will break ranks, though nations trek from progress.
Courage was mine, and I had mystery;
Wisdom was mine, and I had mastery:

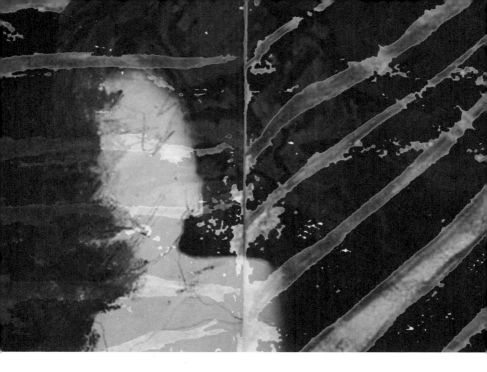

To miss the march of this retreating world
Into vain citadels that are not walled.
Then, when much blood had clogged their chariot-wheels,
I would go up and wash them from sweet wells,
Even with truths that lie too deep for taint.
I would have poured my spirit without stint
But not through wounds; not on the cess of war.
Foreheads of men have bled where no wounds were.

"I am the enemy you killed, my friend.
I knew you in this dark: for so you frowned
Yesterday through me as you jabbed and killed.
I parried; but my hands were loath and cold.
Let us sleep now …"

Illustration: Jennifer Leach

Mental Cases

Who are these? Why sit they here in twilight?
Wherefore rock they, purgatorial shadows,
Drooping tongues from jaws that slob their relish,
Baring teeth that leer like skulls' tongues wicked?
Stroke on stroke of pain, — but what slow panic,
Gouged these chasms round their fretted sockets?
Ever from their hair and through their hand palms
Misery swelters. Surely we have perished
Sleeping, and walk hell; but who these hellish?
— These are men whose minds the Dead have ravished.
Memory fingers in their hair of murders,
Multitudinous murders they once witnessed.
Wading sloughs of flesh these helpless wander,
Treading blood from lungs that had loved laughter.
Always they must see these things and hear them,
Batter of guns and shatter of flying muscles,
Carnage incomparable and human squander
Rucked too thick for these men's extrication.
Therefore still their eyeballs shrink tormented
Back into their brains, because on their sense
Sunlight seems a bloodsmear; night comes blood-black;
Dawn breaks open like a wound that bleeds afresh
— Thus their heads wear this hilarious, hideous,
Awful falseness of set-smiling corpses.
— Thus their hands are plucking at each other;
Picking at the rope-knouts of their scourging;
Snatching after us who smote them, brother,
Pawing us who dealt them war and madness.

A Terre

(Being the philosophy of many Soldiers.)

Sit on the bed; I'm blind, and three parts shell,
Be careful; can't shake hands now; never shall.
Both arms have mutinied against me — brutes.
My fingers fidget like ten idle brats.

I tried to peg out soldierly — no use!
One dies of war like any old disease.
This bandage feels like pennies on my eyes.
I have my medals? — Discs to make eyes close.
My glorious ribbons? — Ripped from my own back
In scarlet shreds. (That's for your poetry book.)

A short life and a merry one, my brick!
We used to say we'd hate to live dead old, —
Yet now . . . I'd willingly be puffy, bald,
And patriotic. Buffers catch from boys
At least the jokes hurled at them. I suppose
Little I'd ever teach a son, but hitting,
Shooting, war, hunting, all the arts of hurting.
Well, that's what I learnt, — that, and making money.
Your fifty years ahead seem none too many?
Tell me how long I've got? God! For one year
To help myself to nothing more than air!
One Spring! Is one too good to spare, too long?
Spring wind would work its own way to my lung,
And grow me legs as quick as lilac-shoots.
My servant's lamed, but listen how he shouts!
When I'm lugged out, he'll still be good for that.
Here in this mummy-case, you know, I've thought
How well I might have swept his floors for ever,
I'd ask no night off when the bustle's over,
Enjoying so the dirt. Who's prejudiced
Against a grimed hand when his own's quite dust,
Less live than specks that in the sun-shafts turn,

THIS BANDAGE feels like PENNIES on my EYES

Illustration: Geoff Sawers

Less warm than dust that mixes with arms' tan?
I'd love to be a sweep, now, black as Town,
Yes, or a muckman. Must I be his load?

O Life, Life, let me breathe, — a dug-out rat!
Not worse than ours the existences rats lead —
Nosing along at night down some safe vat,
They find a shell-proof home before they rot.
Dead men may envy living mites in cheese,
Or good germs even. Microbes have their joys,
And subdivide, and never come to death,
Certainly flowers have the easiest time on earth.
"I shall be one with nature, herb, and stone."
Shelley would tell me. Shelley would be stunned;
The dullest Tommy hugs that fancy now.
"Pushing up daisies," is their creed, you know.
To grain, then, go my fat, to buds my sap,
For all the usefulness there is in soap.
D'you think the Boche will ever stew man-soup?
Some day, no doubt, if ...
                              Friend, be very sure
I shall be better off with plants that share
More peaceably the meadow and the shower.
Soft rains will touch me, — as they could touch once,
And nothing but the sun shall make me ware.
Your guns may crash around me. I'll not hear;
Or, if I wince, I shall not know I wince.
Don't take my soul's poor comfort for your jest.
Soldiers may grow a soul when turned to fronds,
But here the thing's best left at home with friends.

My soul's a little grief, grappling your chest,
To climb your throat on sobs; easily chased
On other sighs and wiped by fresher winds.

Carry my crying spirit till it's weaned
To do without what blood remained these wounds.

The Next War

War's a joke for me and you,
While we know such dreams are true.
— Siegfried Sassoon

Out there, we've walked quite friendly up to Death,—
Sat down and eaten with him, cool and bland,—
Pardoned his spilling mess-tins in our hand.
We've sniffed the green thick odour of his breath,—
Our eyes wept, but our courage didn't writhe.
He's spat at us with bullets and he's coughed
Shrapnel. We chorussed when he sang aloft,
We whistled while he shaved us with his scythe.
Oh, Death was never enemy of ours!
We laughed at him, we leagued with him, old chum.
No soldier's paid to kick against His powers.
We laughed, —knowing that better men would come,
And greater wars: when each proud fighter brags
He wars on Death, for lives; not men, for flags.

Illustration: Sally Castle

Illustration: Terry Cree

S.I.W.

> I will to the King,
> And offer him consolation in his trouble,
> For that man there has set his teeth to die,
> And being one that hates obedience,
> Discipline, and orderliness of life,
> I cannot mourn him.
> — W.B. Yeats

I. The Prologue

Patting good-bye, doubtless they told the lad
He'd always show the Hun a brave man's face;
Father would sooner him dead than in disgrace,—
Was proud to see him going, aye, and glad.
Perhaps his mother whimpered how she'd fret
Until he got a nice safe wound to nurse.
Sisters would wish girls too could shoot, charge, curse ...
Brothers—would send his favourite cigarette.
Each week, month after month, they wrote the same,
Thinking him sheltered in some Y.M. Hut,
Because he said so, writing on his butt
Where once an hour a bullet missed its aim
And misses teased the hunger of his brain.
His eyes grew old with wincing, and his hand
Reckless with ague. Courage leaked, as sand
From the best sand-bags after years of rain.
But never leave, wound, fever, trench-foot, shock,
Untrapped the wretch. And death seemed still withheld
For torture of lying machinally shelled,
At the pleasure of this world's Powers who'd run amok.

He'd seen men shoot their hands, on night patrol.
Their people never knew. Yet they were vile.
'Death sooner than dishonour, that's the style!'
So Father said.

II. The Action

One dawn, our wire patrol
Carried him. This time, Death had not missed.
We could do nothing but wipe his bleeding cough.
Could it be accident? - Rifles go off...
Not sniped? No. (Later they found the English ball.)

III. The Poem

It was the reasoned crisis of his soul
Against more days of inescapable thrall,
Against infrangibly wired and blind trench wall
Curtained with fire, roofed in with creeping fire,
Slow grazing fire, that would not burn him whole
But kept him for death's promises and scoff,
And life's half-promising, and both their riling.

IV. The Epilogue

With him they buried the muzzle his teeth had kissed,
And truthfully wrote the Mother, 'Tim died smiling'.

The Show

My soul looked down from a vague height with Death,
As unremembering how I rose or why,
And saw a sad land, weak with sweats of dearth,
Gray, cratered like the moon with hollow woe,
And fitted with great pocks and scabs of plaques.

Across its beard, that horror of harsh wire,
There moved thin caterpillars, slowly uncoiled.
It seemed they pushed themselves to be as plugs
Of ditches, where they writhed and shrivelled, killed.

By them had slimy paths been trailed and scraped
Round myriad warts that might be little hills.

From gloom's last dregs these long-strung creatures crept,
And vanished out of dawn down hidden holes.

(And smell came up from those foul openings
As out of mouths, or deep wounds deepening.)

On dithering feet upgathered, more and more,
Brown strings towards strings of gray, with bristling spines,
All migrants from green fields, intent on mire.

Those that were gray, of more abundant spawns,
Ramped on the rest and ate them and were eaten.

I saw their bitten backs curve, loop, and straighten,
I watched those agonies curl, lift, and flatten.

Whereat, in terror what that sight might mean,
I reeled and shivered earthward like a feather.

And Death fell with me, like a deepening moan.
And He, picking a manner of worm, which half had hid
Its bruises in the earth, but crawled no further,
Showed me its feet, the feet of many men,
And the fresh-severed head of it, my head.

Disabled

He sat in a wheeled chair, waiting for dark,
And shivered in his ghastly suit of grey,
Legless, sewn short at elbow. Through the park
Voices of boys rang saddening like a hymn,
Voices of play and pleasure after day,
Till gathering sleep had mothered them from him.

*

About this time Town used to swing so gay
When glow-lamps budded in the light-blue trees,
And girls glanced lovelier as the air grew dim,—
In the old times, before he threw away his knees.
Now he will never feel again how slim
Girls' waists are, or how warm their subtle hands,
All of them touch him like some queer disease.

*

There was an artist silly for his face,
For it was younger than his youth, last year.
Now, he is old; his back will never brace;
He's lost his colour very far from here,
Poured it down shell-holes till the veins ran dry,
And half his lifetime lapsed in the hot race
And leap of purple spurted from his thigh.

*

One time he liked a blood-smear down his leg,
After the matches carried shoulder-high.
It was after football, when he'd drunk a peg,
He thought he'd better join. He wonders why.
Someone had said he'd look a god in kilts.
That's why; and maybe, too, to please his Meg,
Aye, that was it, to please the giddy jilts,
He asked to join. He didn't have to beg;
Smiling they wrote his lie: aged nineteen years.

Illustration: Jenny Halstead   25

Germans he scarcely thought of, all their guilt,
And Austria's, did not move him. And no fears
Of Fear came yet. He thought of jewelled hilts
For daggers in plaid socks; of smart salutes;
And care of arms; and leave; and pay arrears;
Esprit de corps; and hints for young recruits.
And soon, he was drafted out with drums and cheers.

*

Some cheered him home, but not as crowds cheer Goal.
Only a solemn man who brought him fruits
Thanked him; and then inquired about his soul.

*

Now, he will spend a few sick years in institutes,
And do what things the rules consider wise,
And take whatever pity they may dole.
Tonight he noticed how the women's eyes
Passed from him to the strong men that were whole.
How cold and late it is! Why don't they come
And put him into bed? Why don't they come?

Exposure

Our brains ache, in the merciless iced east winds that knive us ...
Wearied we keep awake because the night is silent ...
Low drooping flares confuse our memory of the salient ...
Worried by silence, sentries whisper, curious, nervous,
    But nothing happens.

Watching, we hear the mad gusts tugging on the wire,
Like twitching agonies of men among its brambles.
Northward, incessantly, the flickering gunnery rumbles,
Far off, like a dull rumour of some other war.
    What are we doing here?

The poignant misery of dawn begins to grow ...
We only know war lasts, rain soaks, and clouds sag stormy.
Dawn massing in the east her melancholy army
Attacks once more in ranks on shivering ranks of grey,
    But nothing happens.

Sudden successive flights of bullets streak the silence.
Less deadly than the air that shudders black with snow,
With sidelong flowing flakes that flock, pause, and renew,
We watch them wandering up and down the wind's nonchalance,
    But nothing happens.

Pale flakes with fingering stealth come feeling for our faces—
We cringe in holes, back on forgotten dreams, and stare, snow-
    dazed,
Deep into grassier ditches. So we drowse, sun-dozed,
Littered with blossoms trickling where the blackbird fusses.
    —Is it that we are dying?

Slowly our ghosts drag home: glimpsing the sunk fires, glozed
With crusted dark-red jewels; crickets jingle there;
For hours the innocent mice rejoice: the house is theirs;

Shutters and doors, all closed: on us the doors are closed,—
We turn back to our dying.

Since we believe not otherwise can kind fires burn;
Now ever suns smile true on child, or field, or fruit.
For God's invincible spring our love is made afraid;
Therefore, not loath, we lie out here; therefore were born,
For love of God seems dying.

Tonight, this frost will fasten on this mud and us,
Shrivelling many hands, and puckering foreheads crisp.
The burying-party, picks and shovels in shaking grasp,
Pause over half-known faces. All their eyes are ice,
But nothing happens.

Illustration: Sally Castle

Asleep

Under his helmet, up against his pack,
After so many days of work and waking,
Sleep took him by the brow and laid him back.

There, in the happy no-time of his sleeping,
Death took him by the heart. There heaved a quaking
Of the aborted life within him leaping,
Then chest and sleepy arms once more fell slack.

And soon the slow, stray blood came creeping
From the intruding lead, like ants on track.

Whether his deeper sleep lie shaded by the shaking
Of great wings, and the thoughts that hung the stars,
High-pillowed on calm pillows of God's making,
Above these clouds, these rains, these sleets of lead,
And these winds' scimitars,
Or whether yet his thin and sodden head
Confuses more and more with the low mould,
His hair being one with the grey grass
Of finished fields, and wire-scrags rusty-old,
Who knows? Who hopes? Who troubles? Let it pass!
He sleeps. He sleeps less tremulous, less cold,
Than we who wake, and waking say Alas!

The Last Laugh

'O Jesus Christ! I'm hit,' he said; and died.
Whether he vainly cursed or prayed indeed,
    The Bullets chirped—In vain, vain, vain!
    Machine-guns chuckled—Tut-tut! Tut-tut!
    And the Big Gun guffawed.

Another sighed,—'O Mother,—mother,—Dad!'
Then smiled at nothing, childlike, being dead.
    And the lofty Shrapnel-cloud
    Leisurely gestured,—Fool!
    And the splinters spat, and tittered.

'My Love!' one moaned. Love-languid seemed his mood,
Till slowly lowered, his whole face kissed the mud.
    And the Bayonets' long teeth grinned;
    Rabbles of Shells hooted and groaned;
    And the Gas hissed.

Illustration: Martin Andrews 33

Illustration: Sally Castle

Smile, Smile, Smile

Head to limp head, the sunk-eyed wounded scanned
Yesterday's *Mail*; the casualties (typed small)
And (large) Vast Booty from our Latest Haul.
Also, they read of Cheap Homes, not yet planned;
"For," said the paper, "when this war is done
The men's first instinct will be making homes.
Meanwhile their foremost need is aerodromes,
It being certain war has just begun.
Peace would do wrong to our undying dead,—
The sons we offered might regret they died
If we got nothing lasting in their stead.
We must be solidly indemnified.
Though all be worthy Victory which all bought.
We rulers sitting in this ancient spot
Would wrong our very selves if we forgot
The greatest glory will be theirs who fought,
Who kept this nation in integrity."
Nation?—The half-limbed readers did not chafe
But smiled at one another curiously
Like secret men who know their secret safe.
(This is the thing they know and never speak,
That England one by one had fled to France
Not many elsewhere now save under France).
Pictures of these broad smiles appear each week,
And people in whose voice real feeling rings
Say: How they smile! They're happy now, poor things.

The Sentry

We'd found an old Boche dug-out, and he knew,
And gave us hell, for shell on frantic shell
Hammered on top, but never quite burst through.
Rain, guttering down in waterfalls of slime
Kept slush waist high, that rising hour by hour,
Choked up the steps too thick with clay to climb.
What murk of air remained stank old, and sour
With fumes of whizz-bangs, and the smell of men
Who'd lived there years, and left their curse in the den,
If not their corpses …

    There we herded from the blast
Of whizz-bangs, but one found our door at last.
Buffeting eyes and breath, snuffing the candles.
And thud! flump! thud! down the steep steps came thumping
And splashing in the flood, deluging muck —
The sentry's body; then his rifle, handles
Of old Boche bombs, and mud in ruck on ruck.
We dredged him up, for killed, until he whined
"O sir, my eyes — I'm blind — I'm blind, I'm blind!"
Coaxing, I held a flame against his lids
And said if he could see the least blurred light
He was not blind; in time he'd get all right.
"I can't," he sobbed. Eyeballs, huge-bulged like squids
Watch my dreams still; but I forgot him there
In posting next for duty, and sending a scout
To beg a stretcher somewhere, and floundering about
To other posts under the shrieking air.

Those other wretches, how they bled and spewed,
And one who would have drowned himself for good, —
I try not to remember these things now.
Let dread hark back for one word only: how
Half-listening to that sentry's moans and jumps,
And the wild chattering of his broken teeth,
Renewed most horribly whenever crumps
Pummelled the roof and slogged the air beneath —
Through the dense din, I say, we heard him shout
"I see your lights!" But ours had long died out.

Insensibility

I.

Happy are men who yet before they are killed
Can let their veins run cold.
Whom no compassion fleers
Or makes their feet
Sore on the alleys cobbled with their brothers.
The front line withers.
But they are troops who fade, not flowers,
For poets' tearful fooling:
Men, gaps for filling:
Losses, who might have fought
Longer; but no one bothers.

Illustration: Jennifer Leach

And some cease feeling
Even themselves or for themselves.
Dullness best solves
The tease and doubt of shelling,
And Chance's strange arithmetic
Comes simpler than the reckoning of their shilling.
They keep no check on armies' decimation.

III.

Happy are these who lose imagination:
They have enough to carry with ammunition.
Their spirit drags no pack.
Their old wounds, save with cold, can not more ache.
Having seen all things red,
Their eyes are rid
Of the hurt of the colour of blood for ever.
And terror's first constriction over,
Their hearts remain small-drawn.
Their senses in some scorching cautery of battle
Now long since ironed,
Can laugh among the dying, unconcerned.

IV.

Happy the soldier home, with not a notion
How somewhere, every dawn, some men attack,
And many sighs are drained.
Happy the lad whose mind was never trained:
His days are worth forgetting more than not.
He sings along the march
Which we march taciturn, because of dusk,
The long, forlorn, relentless trend
From larger day to huger night.

V

We wise, who with a thought besmirch
Blood over all our soul,
How should we see our task
But through his blunt and lashless eyes?
Alive, he is not vital overmuch;
Dying, not mortal overmuch;
Nor sad, nor proud,
Nor curious at all.
He cannot tell
Old men's placidity from his.

VI.

But cursed are dullards whom no cannon stuns,
That they should be as stones.
Wretched are they, and mean
With paucity that never was simplicity.
By choice they made themselves immune
To pity and whatever moans in man
Before the last sea and the hapless stars;
Whatever mourns when many leave these shores;
Whatever shares
The eternal reciprocity of tears.

Afterword

The first son of Tom and Susan Owen, Wilfred Edward Salter Owen was born on 18 March 1893 in Oswestry, Shropshire, and grew up in Birkenhead and Shrewsbury. He was educated at the Birkenhead Institute and Shrewsbury Borough Technical School, and for a time worked as a Temporary Pupil Teacher at Wyle Cop School in Shrewsbury, but he was not enamoured with the idea of being a schoolmaster. He dreamed of going to Oxford, but as the son of a railway superintendent, his university aspirations were checked by a lack of money and influence. He embarked instead on a course of private study for matriculation at University College London. While he passed the gruelling examination, it was not with the first-class honours required to win a scholarship.

Thus in 1911, his hopes for university dashed, he became lay assistant to the vicar of Dunsden parish, near where his maternal cousins the Gunstons lived. Such an appointment pleased his mother Susan greatly, a devout evangelical woman with whom he remained extremely close his entire life, who nurtured hopes of a career in the Church for her eldest son. In exchange for help with parish work, Owen was given board and lodging, and the Reverend Herbert Wigan promised to tutor him in preparation for another university entrance exam. Parish work dominated the young lay assistant's time. He visited the sick, conducted children's services and Scripture Union meetings, and found he was good at public speaking: 'I use no notes, and spend no great time in preparation; but I use no high falutin' words, but try to express myself in simple, straightforward English.' He delighted in the company of the young in the village whom he referred to as 'my children', but the vicar's academic coaching left Owen wanting. No great lover of literature, Wigan offered to teach Greek and Hebrew, 'all Theological dustiness', 'a shifting, hypothetical, doubt-fostering, dusty and unprofitable study'.

To the rescue came Miss Edith Morley. Owen had been attending botany classes at University College Reading and his lecturer, realising his student's literary aspirations, recommended a visit to the Head of the English Department. Described by Dominic Hibberd as a 'burly and deep-voiced' and 'formidable character, devoted to her students though often tiresome to her colleagues' (Hibberd, 2002), Edith Morley was the first female professor in the country, having been elevated to the post in 1908. She recognised in the young Wilfred Owen an 'unhappy adolescent, suffering badly from lack of understanding … and in need of encouragement and praise', and invited him to attend her classes. She also gave him 'useful advice about the technicalities of poetry' (Stallworthy, 1974), and encouraged him in writing his own poems, drafts of which he sent to her from time to time.

Owen clearly cherished Morley's advice and sympathetic encouragement during his stay at Dunsden, where the grinding poverty of many in the village weighed more heavily on him each day. What Owen called 'the wretched hovels' and the 'crazy, evil-smelling huts' of the poor contrasted sharply with the comforts and genteel society of the vicarage. The sympathy and pity that would characterise his feelings for his men during the War was partly born in Dunsden. As he began 'increasingly liberalizing and liberating my thought', his situation and his health began deteriorating. With his nerves 'in a shocking state', and needing to 'escape from this hotbed of religion', Owen returned to Shrewsbury, where his family doctor suggested that the warmer climate of southern France might do him good.

Still searching for a profession, and with his hopes of university as well as a career in the Church behind him, Owen took up a post as part-time English teacher with the Berlitz School Bordeaux. He was working as an English tutor in the spa town of Bagnères-de-Bigorre in the La Gailleste valley at the foot of the Pyrenees when war broke out in 1914. Enjoying the company of the Léger family and the tutelage of the French poet Laurent Tailhaide, the outbreak of war initially affected Owen 'less than it ought' for, as he wrote to his mother, 'I can do no service to anybody by agitating for news or making dole over the slaughter.' But his attitude changed and by June 1915 he informed his mother that he 'intensely' wanted 'to fight'. Owen enlisted in the Artists' Rifles in October 1915, was commissioned second lieutenant in the Manchester Regiment in 1916, and trained variously in London and the north of England before embarking for active service in January 1917.

The initial 'fine heroic feeling about being in France' and his 'perfect spirits', changed quickly once Owen joined his regiment, the 2nd Manchesters at Halloy, near Beaumont Hamel, which had just been involved in severe fighting: 'We were let down, gently, into the real thing, Mud. [...] I am perfectly well and strong, but unthinkably dirty and squalid.' Owen's letters from the Western Front in that winter and spring of 1917 are palimpsests of his poems. Immediate and raw, they are testaments to Owen's power of vivid description, his mastery of cadence and sound, and his skill at the slow accretion of detail so characteristic of his poetry, as in this letter of 16 January 1917:

> I can see no excuse for deceiving you about these last 4 days. I have suffered seventh hell.
>
> I have not been at the front.
>
> I have been at the front of it.
>
> I held an advanced post, that is, a 'dug-out' in the middle of No Man's Land.
>
> We had march of 3 miles over shelled road then nearly 3 along a flooded trench. After that we came to where the trenches had been blown flat out and had to go over the top. It was of course dark, too dark, and the ground was not mud, not sloppy mud, but an octopus of sucking clay, 3, 4, and 5 feet deep, relieved only by craters full of water. Men have been known to drown in them. Many stuck in the mud & only got on by leaving their waders, equipment, and in some cases their clothes.
>
> High explosives were dropping all around out, and machine guns spluttered every few minutes. But it was so dark that even the German flares did not reveal us.
>
> Three quarters dead, I mean each of us 3/4 dead, we reached the dug-out, and relieved the wretches therein. I then had to go forth and find another dug-out for a still more advanced post where I left 18 bombers. I was responsible for other posts on the left but there was a junior officer in charge.
>
> My dug-out held 25 men tight packed. Water filled it to a depth of 1 or 2 feet, leaving say 4 feet of air.
>
> One entrance had been blown in & blocked.
>
> So far, the other remained.
>
> The Germans knew we were staying there and decided we shouldn't.

Those fifty hours were the agony of my happy life.

Every ten minutes on Sunday afternoon seemed an hour.

I nearly broke down and let myself drown in the water that was now slowly rising over my knees.

The source of 'The Sentry' is found here:

In the Platoon on my left the sentries over the dug-out were blown to nothing. One of these poor fellows was my first servant whom I rejected. If I had kept him he would have lived, for servants don't do Sentry Duty. I kept my own sentries half way down the stairs during the more terrific bombardment. In spite of this one lad was blown down and, I am afraid, blinded.

Diagnosed with neurasthenia, initially as a result of concussion in March, and then, in April, from being blown into a railway cutting where he lay next to a dead officer for several days, Owen was sent, via the Royal Victoria Hospital, Netley, to Craiglockhart Military Hospital, Edinburgh, for treatment. Here, under the treatment of Dr Arthur Brock RAMC and with the encouragement of Siegfried Sassoon (remembered by posterity as one of the greatest and most influential friendships in literary history), Owen learned how to channel his nightmarish memories of the Western Front into poems such as those featured in this volume.

The title, *Pennies on my Eyes,* is a phrase from 'A Terre', quoted less often than 'Anthem for Doomed Youth', 'Dulce et Decorum Est' or 'Strange Meeting', but as in these more familiar poems, the distinctive voice of Wilfred Owen rings clear; the use of pararhyme, the striking imagery, the language resonant of many influences – the Bible, the Romantic poets, contemporary slang, and Sassoon. Owen turns the custom of placing coins on the eyelids of a corpse to keep them closed into an unmistakable image of the Great War: 'The bandage feels like pennies on my eyes./ I have my medals?—Discs to make my eyes close' (ll. 7-8). If satire is here, 'My glorious ribbons?—Ripped from my own back/In scarlet shreds. (That's for your poetry book.)' (ll. 9-10), so is pity. Always pity: 'Don't take my soul's poor comfort for your jest' (l. 58).

'A Terre' was written and revised in what might be called Owen's *annus mirabilis*, the period between resuming military service in the

Autumn of 1917 after his treatment at Craiglockhart and his death on the Sambre–Oise canal at Ors just a week before the Armistice. Whilst stationed at Scarborough as camp commandant/major-domo to the officers of the 5th (Reserve) Battalion at the Clarence Gardens Hotel, Owen wrote to his mother Susan on 3 December 1917: 'I finished an important poem this afternoon', and three days later wrote to Sassoon that 'This "Wild with all Regrets" was begun & ended two days ago, at one gasp. If simplicity, if imaginativeness, if sympathy, if resonance of vowels, make poetry I have not succeeded. But if you say "Here is poetry," it will be so for me'. 'Wild with all Regrets' was expanded into 'A Terre' in April 1918, whilst Owen was stationed at the Northern Command Depot at Ripon. Here, in a little attic room he had rented at 7 Borage Lane, getting physically fit and 'completely restituted from Shell Shock', he wrote and revised such poems as 'Insensibility', 'Strange Meeting', 'Exposure', and 'Futility'. By New Year's Eve he was able to declare to Susan:

> I am not dissatisfied with my years. Everything has been done in bouts:

> Bouts of awful labour at Shrewsbury & Bordeaux; bouts of amazing pleasure in the Pyrenees, and play at Craiglockhart; bouts of religion at Dunsden; bouts of horrible danger on the Somme; bouts of poetry always; of your affection always; of sympathy for the oppressed always.

> I go out of this year a Poet, my dear Mother, as which I did not enter it. I am held peer by the Georgians; I am a poet's poet.

Wilfred Owen the poet we know today was virtually unknown in his own lifetime, except to a coterie of literary figures, including Sassoon, Robert Graves, C.K. Scott Moncrieff and Osbert Sitwell, and to readers of *The Bookman* and *The Nation*, periodicals which published the only five poems he saw in print. But Owen's posthumous reputation grew steadily at the hands of editors who were also poets: *Poems* by Wilfred Owen (1920), edited by Edith Sitwell with an introduction by Siegfried Sassoon; *The Poems of Wilfred Owen* (1931) edited with a memoir and notes by Edmund Blunden; *The Collected Poems of Wilfred Owen* (1963), edited by Cecil Day Lewis and including nineteen previously unpublished poems; and *The Complete Poems and Fragments* (edited by Jon Stallworthy, 1983/2013). In 1962, Benjamin Britten incorporated

Owen's poems into *War Requiem*, composed to consecrate the new Coventry Cathedral, one of the symbols of the destruction caused by yet another world war. The publication of the *Collected Letters* (edited by Harold Owen and John Bell, 1967), three major biographies (Stallworthy, 1974/2013; Hibberd, 2009; Cuthbertson 2014), and numerous critical studies have cemented Owen's reputation in the literary canon. Publications such as this volume, however, demonstrate how Owen's poems continue to inspire the work of other artists, here those who create in images rather than words. In this volume's pages we see everything from disquiet at patriotic rhetoric and enlistment enthusiasm ('Anthem for Doomed Youth', 'Dulce et Decorum Est', 'The Send-Off'); comradeship and harrowing battle ('Exposure', 'The Show', and 'Spring Offensive'); the living hell of physical and psychological wounds ('Disabled', 'Mental Cases'); to death, ghosts, and descents into the underworld ('Asleep', 'Strange Meeting').

Pennies on my Eyes, with its contributions by local artists from Reading, a town that was central to Owen's literary and personal development – however uncomfortable that may have been as he matured – vividly shows that despite being rooted in the cataclysm of 1914–18, Owen's themes transcend his own historical period. And it goes some way to reinforcing his hope that his 'elegies', if to his generation were 'in no sense consolatory', remain evocative and resonant 'to the next'.

Jane Potter

Bibliography

Guy Cuthbertson, *Wilfred Owen* (2014), Yale University Press

Dominic Hibberd, *Wilfred Owen: A New Biography* (2002), Weidenfeld & Nicolson

Wilfred Owen, *The Complete Poems and Fragments*, 2 vols. (1983/2013), ed. Jon Stallworthy, Oxford University Press

Wilfred Owen, *Selected Letters* (1998), ed. John Bell, Oxford University Press

Jane Potter, *Wilfred Owen: An Illustrated Life* (2014), Bodleian Library Publishing

Jon Stallworthy, *Wilfred Owen* (1974/2013), Oxford University Press

Biographies of artists

Ahmad Alazami

Ahmad Alazami is a Syrian artist, born and raised in Damascus and currently living in Reading with his wife and two boys. He graduated in Fine Arts in Syria but had to flee the country after going through many difficulties. He has used his art to express the pain and suffering he saw amongst his compatriots who are trying to survive a terrifying crisis. To do this he has created a new technique that incorporates nails, string, inked Arabic calligraphy and lighting, which gives the art a multi-dimensional aspect.

Martin Andrews

Martin Andrews was a student of Fine Art at the University of Reading and later transferred to graduate in Typography & Graphic Communication. For many years he was a museum and exhibition designer before returning to the University to be a lecturer in the Department of Typography. As well as studio teaching, he became a printing historian and has published widely and lectured in this country and abroad. Since retirement from the University, Martin has concentrated on painting, printmaking and illustration and continues to write and publish on a variety of subjects. He is a past president of the Reading Guild of Artists and exhibits his paintings and prints regularly. He has been part of Two Rivers Press for many years and is one of their authors and illustrators.

Sally Castle

Sally Castle is a designer and illustrator with a reputation for original hand lettering, and a particular interest in linocut printmaking and environmental lettering –most notable works so far in this area are the Walking Words panels at Chatham Place in Reading, the Forbury Square stone in Reading and village signs. A commission in 2009 for The University of Reading Carrington building resulted in a large scale linocut print. Design for print has included book design and illustration and all kinds of printed matter as well as individual commissions. She has illustrated over thirty book covers and especially enjoys illustrating poetry books. Sally has been a member of Two Rivers Press for over twenty years.

Terry Cree

Terry Cree is a writer and artist living in Shropshire. He is the author of one book of poems published by Two Rivers Press and is currently working on a sculpture garden and a collection of 400 stories.

Nadja Guggi

Nadja Guggi is an artist and designer based in Wiltshire, where she runs creative studio Messrs. Dash & Dare. A design graduate of the University of Reading, she lived and worked in the town for almost 20 years, and has been part of Two Rivers Press as one its designers and illustrators for over a decade.

Jenny Halstead

Jenny Halstead studied Fine Art in London before training in medical illustration, working with surgeons and anatomists in teaching hospitals and on publications. She has since moved through the world of dinosaurs and natural history and come full circle, back to painting. She has been Artist in Residence in the Harris Garden in the University of Reading and at the archaeological site at Silchester, producing books on both projects, which were published by Two Rivers Press.

Jennifer Leach

Jennifer Leach is an artist, writer, director of arts company Outrider Anthems and of Reading's recent Festival of the Dark. Her interest lies in the sanctity and energy of creativity, and in its unique power to burst open our small minds to the riches and challenges of the greater universe. She is increasingly exploring ways to engage human beings in 'Conversations at the End of Time'. Jennifer is also co-founder and co-Chair of the Dunsden Owen Association.

Geoff Sawers

Geoff Sawers trained as an artist; subsequent careers as a barman, postman and man all foundered, but he has written and illustrated several books and maps for Two Rivers Press and The Literary Gift Company. A house-husband with three young children, he divides his time between the gutter and the stars.

Two Rivers Press has been publishing in and about Reading since 1994. Founded by the artist Peter Hay (1951–2003), the press continues to delight readers, local and further afield, with its varied list of individually designed, thought-provoking books.

The poems in this collection are set in Janson – a lively modern revival of a traditional serif typeface with high stroke contrast and a large x-height to aid legibility. For the headings, we've used Parisine, a contemporary sanserif, to provide a counterpoint to the classic feel of Janson.